THE GHOSTLY TALES OF THE HAUNTED NORTH CAROLINA COAST

Published by Arcadia Children's Books
A Division of Arcadia Publishing, Inc.
Charleston, SC
www.arcadiapublishing.com

First published 2025
Manufactured in the United States

Designed by Jessica Nevins
Images used courtesy of Shutterstock.com; p. 44 Thomas T. Waterman/ File:Mcdowell at chowan.jpg/Wikimedia Commons/Public domain; p. 64 Jean Leon Gerome Ferris/ File:Capture-of-Blackbeard.jpg/Wikimedia Commons/Public domain; p. 96 LEE SNIDER PHOTO IMAGES/Shutterstock.com.

Sources:
https://blogs.loc.gov/headlinesandheroes/2023/01/the-mysterious-disappearance-of-ghost-ship-carroll-a-deerings-crew/
https://www.youtube.com/watch?v=Nl7oZEuYb8M&t=13s

ISBN: 9781467197991
Library of Congress Control Number: 2025932959

Spooky America

The Ghostly Tales of the Haunted North Carolina Coast

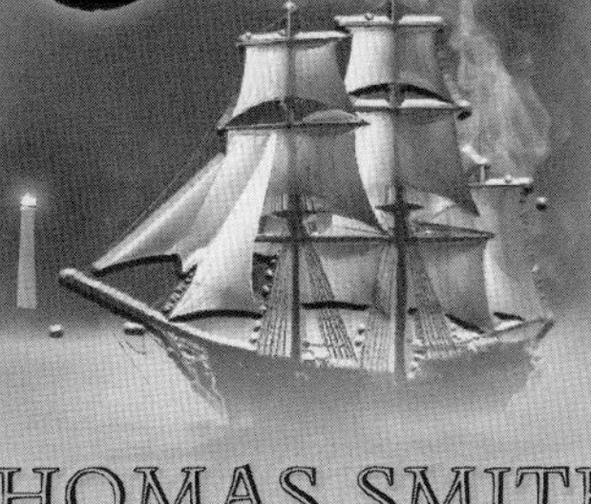

Thomas Smith

Adapted from *Haunted North Carolina Coast* by Thomas Smith

arcadia
CHILDREN'S BOOKS

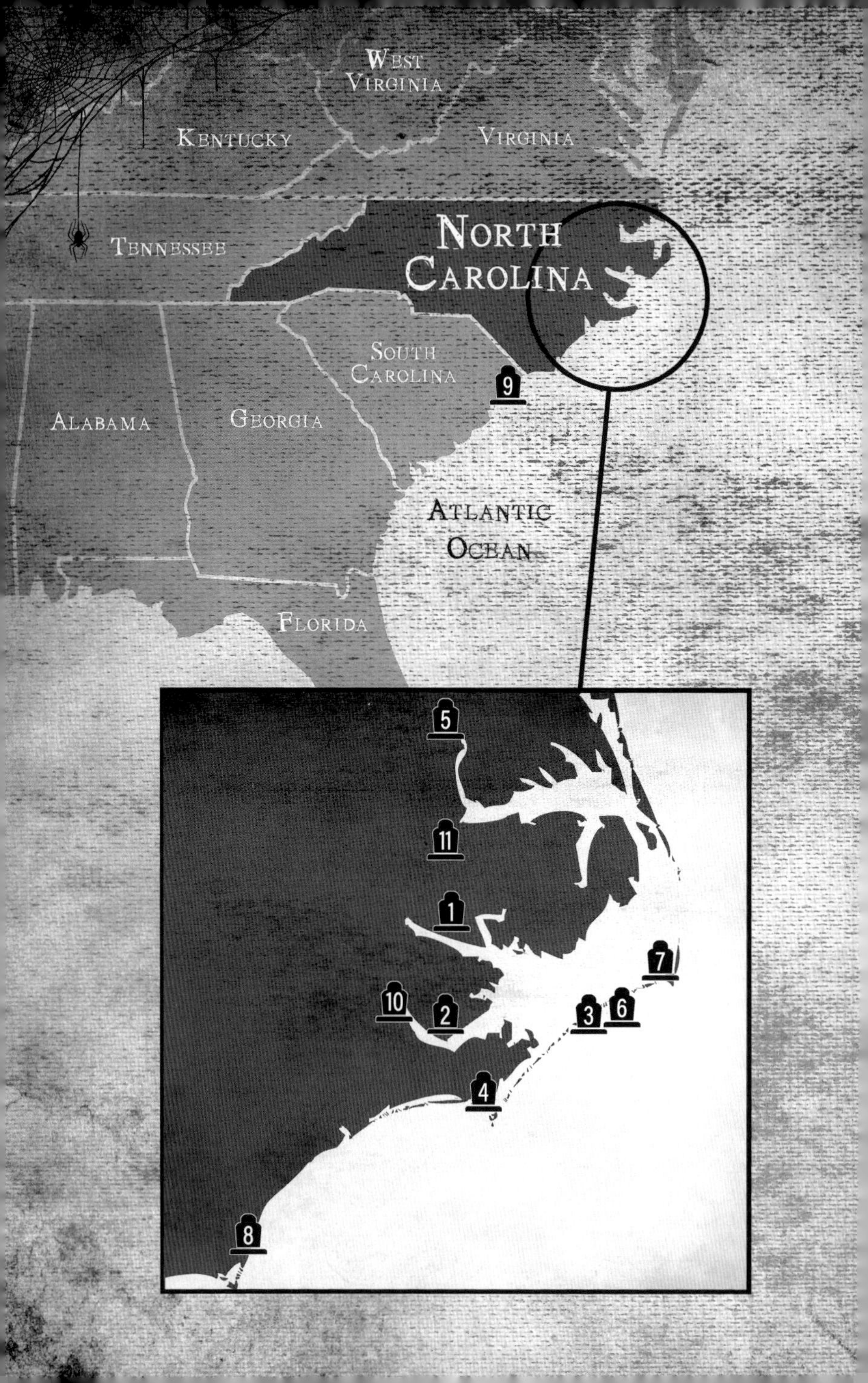
West Virginia
Kentucky
Virginia
Tennessee
North Carolina
South Carolina
Alabama
Georgia
Atlantic Ocean
Florida
9
5
11
1
7
10
2
3
6
4
8

Table of Contents & Map Key

Author's Note

When I was about seven years old, I lived in the country beside a dirt road. About a quarter mile down that dirt road stood an old, run-down, rickety house. An old, run-down, rickety *haunted* house. Everyone knew about it, but nobody really talked about it. Now, like any self-respecting seven-year-old, I was part of a club. And what do you think the club initiation was?

Exactly.

You had to walk down to the haunted house and knock on the front door three times. And

I'm here to tell you the trip back up the road after that third knock was *MUCH* faster than the original trip down to the house. But if you were going to be a member of the Ghost Hunters Club (I never said we were terribly original), you had to knock on that door.

After that, our secret meetings consisted of roasting hot dogs or marshmallows in the backyard and telling scary stories as it was getting dark.

A few years later, my family moved to a new town. And just like every self-respecting town in America, this one had a haunted house. As the story is told, old man Scrimshaw lost his mind one night, killed his family (everybody except the family dog), and then took his own life. Afterward, on the night of the full moon, people said you could hear screams and the howl of a dog coming from the house.

Since my father was a minister, we moved

to a new town every four or five years. With every new town, there was a new haunted house, an eerie abandoned school, or an unexplained phenomenon that appeared on a semi-regular basis—and I couldn't get enough. The stranger it was, the more I wanted to see it. Or at least *read* about it. Between the school library, public library, and the bookmobile, I read dozens of books of ghost stories. Ghosts from the mountains, the coast, the piedmont, small towns, and large cities. Like I said, I just couldn't get enough.

When I got older, I went off to college and found people like me who also loved ghost stories and creepy places. Now that we could drive (hooray!!), we took trips to haunted houses, haunted battlegrounds, and towns that had ghost tours—places where unexplained occurrences were almost commonplace. We saw the hoofprints at Bath (that story is just a few pages away). The Devil's Tramping Ground. The Maco lights. Haunted trains. And a few places where not much happened, but we still managed to creep each other out telling spooky stories.

Then I "grew up" (okay, that depends on who you ask) and became a writer. And what did I write about? Mostly scary things. I wrote scary short stories, plays, books, screenplays, and even lived in a haunted house in Georgia for a few years. (Fortunately, the ghost and I got along okay, so that was good.)

Today, I live at the beach, where I write scary stuff for some really great publishers (like the one who published this book). Sometimes, while I write, my wife sits in the next room reading mystery novels. Every now and then, I hear her get the binoculars from the table by her chair. You see, we live right by the ocean, and my wife loves watching cruise ships. On days when the cruise ships leave the port, she watches them through the binoculars for a few minutes. She likes to see which ships are sailing away and where they're going. Sometimes she even spots one of the new super-huge ships—those are impressive! Then she starts dreaming about which cruise we should take next.

But here's a secret: I use those binoculars, too. Late at night, when everyone else is sleeping and the moon is just right, I pick them up and look out at the dark ocean. But I'm not searching for cruise ships. Oh no, I'm looking for something *much* more mysterious...

I'm looking for ghost ships manned by their long-dead crews.

Just like the ones in this book.

So, as we used to say in the Ghost Hunters Club: *Hey, do you want to hear something spooky?*

Welcome to the Spooky North Carolina Coast!

Why is the North Carolina coast so haunted?

That's an excellent question! I'm glad you asked.

The truth is, it would be difficult for the coast of North Carolina *not* to be haunted. Between the graveyards, pirates, sunken ships, duels, murders, unexplained events, sinister lighthouses, and even a race against the devil (we'll get to that in a few minutes), it would be more surprising if the coast *wasn't* haunted! Take the graveyards for example.

On Ocracoke Island, there are eighty-three cemeteries. Not bad for an island only 9.6 miles long. And that includes public cemeteries, family graveyards, and a military cemetery. That's right. There are four British Royal Navy sailors buried in the Ocracoke British Cemetery. Their bodies washed up on shore after their ship, the HMT *Bedfordshire*, was sunk by a torpedo off the coast of North Carolina during World War II. In fact, so many ships were sunk by German submarines during the war that the area was called Torpedo Alley. All thirty-seven crewmembers were killed, but only four bodies were ever recovered.

In the community cemetery at Sunset Village, many people have seen an older ghostly couple dressed in nineteenth-century clothes. And on a different part of the island, Fannie Pearl MacWilliams Wahab's grave is marked with a *No Trespassing* sign because so many people wanted to have a paranormal experience there (more about her later, too). Add to that all of the unmarked graves of pirates, enslaved people, and shipwrecked sailors, and you have the beginnings of a haunted coast.

Now, let's move along to Springer's Point Nature Preserve. It's a beautiful place during the day. You can walk through the maritime forest, see majestic red cedars, visit the salt marsh, and maybe even have a picnic on the sound-front beach. But it would be best if you were packed up and gone before nightfall. Unless, of course, you want to run into the large, bearded ghost on one of the paths leading out of the reserve. He doesn't just stand on the path and look scary—he will run after you! One local musician, now deceased (maybe he's out there, too . . . who knows), told for years about the bearded ghost who chased him through the woods at Springer's Point, all the way to the sound, before vanishing in a cloud of smoke.

Springer's Point was also one of the legendary pirate Blackbeard's favorite hideouts. In fact, after a three-day pirate gathering full of feasting and singing at the point, the terrifying pirate was finally caught and beheaded. Some people say his headless ghost is still at Springer's Point, looking for his missing head! But we'll talk more about Blackbeard and his cohorts a little later.

The North Carolina coast is home to some amazing ghost ships. There's the mysterious *Carroll A. Deering* and a glowing spectral vessel known as the Flaming Ship of Ocracoke. We even have a famous battleship from World War II that is now a museum you can visit. It's called the Battleship North Carolina. Some say a few ghost sailors still walk its passageways, watching over their old ship.

Then there are the inns, hotels, and bars along the coast. Places where former patrons return from beyond the grave to wander the hallways, move items, and otherwise cling to their previous lives. There are stately homes where the original owners, though long dead, still roam.

There's even a haunted town. Here, the historical society has a ghost tour with over twenty stops along the way. They'll be happy to take you to every haunted site and tell you the chilling tales at each one.

If you're brave enough.

But beware. The citizens of Murfreesboro still keep a few of its secrets to themselves.

You see, the coast of North Carolina is full of "ghoulies and ghosties and long-leggedy beasties, and things that go bump in the night." And just in case that doesn't answer the question of why the coast of North Carolina is such a haunted place, don't worry. We're just getting started.

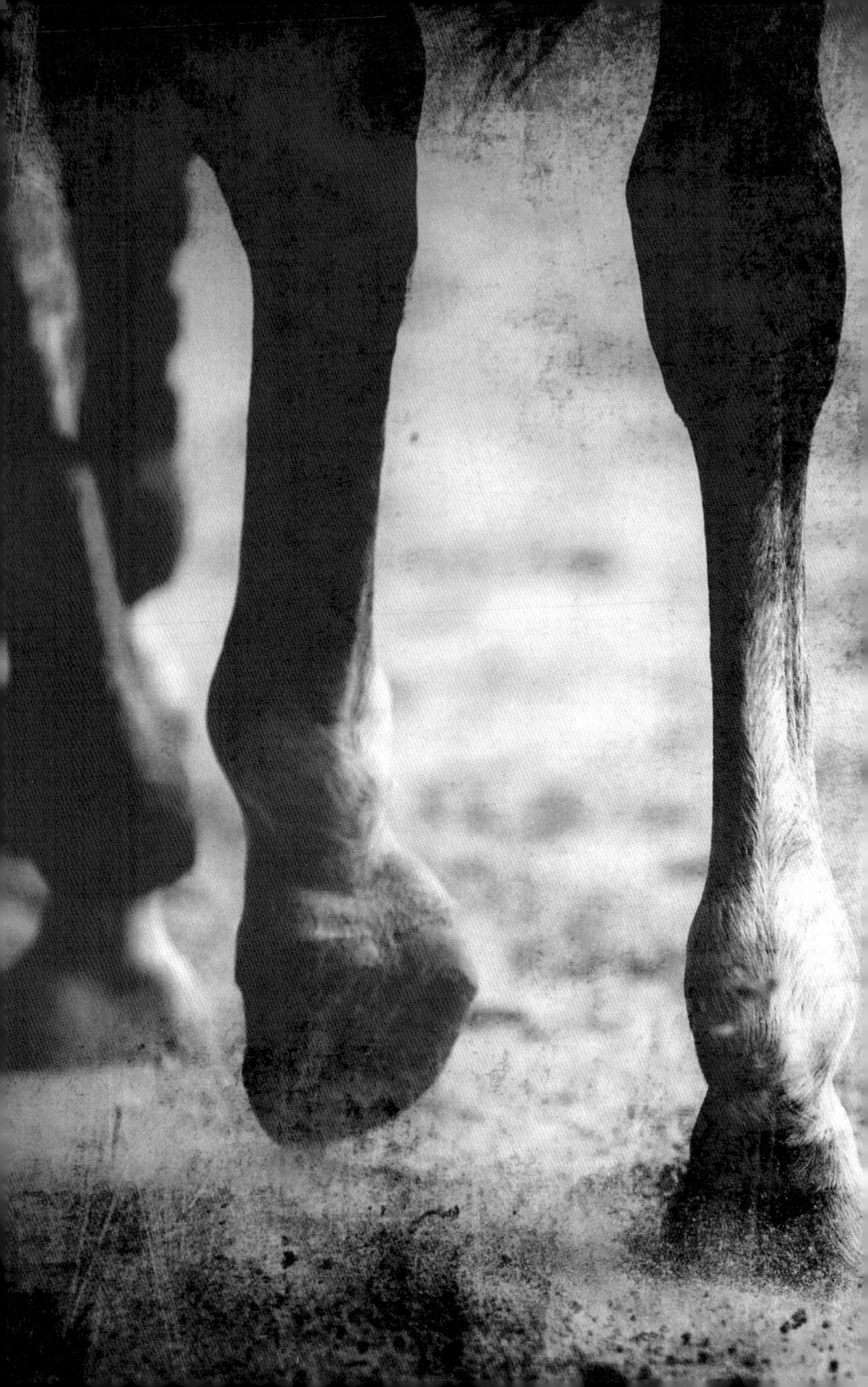

CHAPTER 1

The Hoofprints at Bath

Jesse Elliot was one of the meanest men in the town of Bath. He was a drinker, a fighter, and a gambler. In fact, the only thing he liked better than drinking, fighting, and gambling was horse racing. Jesse would take on all comers. Anytime, and any place, for any stakes. And since Jesse had one of the best horses in the county, if somebody wanted to bet on a race, he was ready to ride.

Even on Sundays.

But on Sunday, October 13, 1813, it would have been better for him to stay home or go to church. The day the stranger in black came to town.

Like he did most days, Jesse Elliot was killing time at the Commons in downtown Bath. He and some friends were talking and bragging about their weekend, and Jesse was bragging more than usual. Everything seemed ordinary until Jesse's dog—his constant companion—began to growl deep in his chest.

The kind of growl that signaled danger. Jesse looked away from his friends and watched as a stranger approached.

The dog continued to growl that low, menacing growl. As Jesse tried to quiet his dog, the animal's hackles began to rise and he lowered his head. The stranger, tall and dressed all in black, seemed not to notice. He just walked up to Jesse and his friends and began to speak.

"Jesse Elliot, I understand you are something of a horseman," the stranger said, his dark eyes flashing. "I also heard you are a betting man."

Jesse winked at his friends, then looked at the man in black. "Well, stranger, it seems you have heard correctly on both counts. That being said, did you come just to make conversation, or do you have a proposition in mind?" Jesse and his friends snickered.

"Oh, I definitely have a proposition for you, Mr. Elliot," the stranger said. He smiled an unsettling smile and took a step forward. "I know you think you have a fast horse, but I believe my horse is much faster. And if you're not afraid, I say we put your boasts to the test."

Jesse sized up the stranger for a moment, then said, "Okay. If it's agreeable to you, I'll go home and get my horse. Then we'll meet at the old town road and see who is the fastest."

The stranger's smile widened, white teeth gleaming, and he nodded in agreement.

Jesse's friends were suddenly not so sure the race was a good idea, but Jesse was already heading toward his home.

Jesse blew into his house like a small hurricane. His wife asked if he had come to go to church with her (just like

she asked every Sunday), and he just pushed past her, took a swig of whiskey, and pulled on his riding boots. Then he ran out to the stable and saddled his chestnut-colored quarter horse. As he was swinging his leg over the saddle, he saw that his dog was still growling and barking.

"Shut up, dog," he yelled, and rode off toward town. Soon, he arrived at the road where the race was to take place and pulled his horse up sharply.

The stranger was riding the most powerful looking horse Jesse had ever seen. The stallion was midnight black and his eyes flashed with an unearthly fire. For the first time in his life, Jesse Elliot was having second thoughts about accepting a challenge to race. But with his friends watching, and that stranger smiling that strange smile, he had no choice. So, Jesse pulled up even with the stranger and waited.

A few seconds later, one of Jesse's friends fired a shot in the air, and the two horses leaped forward. Hooves pounded and dirt flew as the two riders raced down the old road. Jesse spurred his horse, pulled ahead of the stranger, and pushed his horse even harder. The large chestnut horse seemed to fly down the road. For the first hundred yards or so,

Jesse didn't dare look back, although he could hear the stranger's horse gaining on them. The thundering hooves pushed the stranger's horse closer and closer. And even so, Jesse had the feeling that the stranger was holding back. Like he was waiting for something.

Jesse looked straight ahead, grit his teeth, and dug his heels in hard. The thundering sound of the eight hooves striking the ground was almost deafening. The landscape was flying by in a blur, and Jesse felt his horse taking in huge lungfuls of air. He also felt the breath from the stranger's horse on his back . . . and heard the stranger laugh.

That's when Jesse realized this was no ordinary race.

He was in a race for his *life*.

Suddenly, Jesse saw the curve in the road just ahead. He knew if he could make it around the bend before the big stallion and keep the lead for less than another minute, he would win the race. In a massive effort, he spurred his horse one last time. The horse responded with a burst of speed unlike anything Jesse had ever experienced. Jesse yelled into the wind, "Either take me a winner, or take me to hell."

In that moment, Jesse's horse turned its head to look behind them, mane flying wildly and foam flying from its mouth. Whatever the horse saw made it halt abruptly. Jesse's horse planted all four hooves on the ground and stopped on the spot. But Jesse was not so lucky. He pitched forward over the horse and hit a pine tree headfirst. He was dead before he hit the ground.

When Jesse's friends arrived at the scene of the accident, there was no rider on a midnight black stallion, just five hoofprints in the dirt. Four belonged to Jesse's horse. To this day, people say the fifth hoofprint belonged to the stranger's horse and was planted there when the stranger took Jesse's soul to hell.

What do you think?

All I know for sure is that the hoofprints are still there today. And all attempts to alter or remove them since 1813 have failed.

CHAPTER 2

Where Are You, My Son?

Love is a wonderful thing. It's one of the strongest forces in the world. We all want to be loved, and we all want someone to love. But be careful. Sometimes love is a stronger force than you might realize. Take, for example, the old blind woman and her son who lived near the swamp, just outside the town of Arapahoe. They lived in an old shack in a dense stand of pines, out where the Neuse River empties into the Pamlico Sound.

Life was hard, but they never complained. There were plenty of fish, crabs, and clams in the waters near the shack. And the boy gathered berries, medicinal roots, and other things from the surrounding woods. The woods were also full of deer, rabbits, quail, and squirrels, all of which kept them fed, and the old woman's son sold the extra fish, game, and herbs to bring in what little money he could. Even though life was hard, their love made the shack a happy home.

Because she was blind, the old woman seldom went far from the cabin. But on those occasions when she did have to go into the yard and beyond, she carried a long stick and tapped it like a cane to help her walk across the uneven ground. Though she sometimes ventured as far as the edge of the woods, she never went into the deep woods—and she *never* tried to walk out to the water. She knew if she needed anything, all she had to do was call out to her son, and he would come to her right away.

If she needed a fire in the hearth, she could call out, "Where are you, my son?" and soon he would be there, building a nice, warm fire. If she wanted him to read to her, she would call out, "Where are you, my son?" and before long,

he would be by her side, reading. No matter where he was or how softly she called, he was so accustomed to listening for his mother's voice that he was able to quickly hear and find her.

Then, one day, a big storm came. The skies seemed to open up, bringing heavy winds and rain to the area for an entire week. While the storm raged, the boy was stuck inside the cabin with his mother, unable to fish, go foraging in the woods, or hunt. When the storm finally ended, the boy rushed outside to return to his usual activities. But the forest floor was muddy and slippery from all the rain, making it hard to track the animals. Still, the boy kept at it and eventually had some luck. Little did he know, when he started walking along the shoreline, his trip would soon take a tragic turn.

Because of the torrential rains, the bank

was unstable. While the boy was setting his fishing net, the bank collapsed, and he fell into the water. The boy was a strong swimmer, but the constant rain had made the current much stronger than usual. And even though he swam as hard as he could, he wasn't strong enough to reach the shore. No matter what he tried, no matter how hard he kicked, the boy was no match for the surging water. Despite his struggle to survive, the current swept him away, and in the end, the river won. It pulled him down, and the young man drowned.

Later that afternoon, the boy's mother became cold and called out for her son to stoke the fire—but there was no response. At first, she was not alarmed. She knew the muddy conditions would most likely slow him down. After about an hour, she became worried and called out every few minutes, "Where are you, my son? Where are you, my son?" Each time, her cries were met with silence. Finally, her fear took over and she made the difficult decision to try to find her son.

She took her long stick and headed out toward the water. But as with her son, things soon took a tragic turn. She became lost in the woods and, without her son to answer her calls, was never able to find her way out. The old woman's body was found a week or so later near the river. But the story doesn't end there.

Long after the cabin was forgotten—the old woman and her son little more than a distant memory—people in the surrounding area reported hearing the sound of tapping and a woman's voice calling, "Where are you, my son? Where are you, my son?"

About seventy years ago, Camp Seagull was built in Arapahoe, North Carolina. The camp is not too far from the site of the shack where the old blind woman and her son once lived. To this day, campers and counselors alike insist that sometimes, when the camp is dark and everyone is in bed, you can hear the sound of something tapping the ground and a voice calling out into the night, "Where are you, my son?" *Tap...tap...tap.* "Where are you, my son?"

CHAPTER 3

Death Dream

Some things are hard—if not impossible—to explain. Take the story of Fannie Pearl MacWilliams Wahab, for example. Born on Ocracoke Island in September 1894 to John and Elizabeth MacWilliams, she grew up within sight of the Ocracoke Lighthouse. Her father owned a collection of retail stores and a dock on the water. Everybody called it the Department Store. In addition to the shops, there was also a school located in the Odd Fellows Lodge. The building was originally built as a lodge for the Independent Order of Odd Fellows. But Ocracoke's K-12 school operated on the first floor until a new school was built in 1917.

This lodge/school was where Fannie Pearl MacWilliams attended school. One of the teachers there was a young man named Robert Stanley Wahab, a native of Ocracoke. The teacher and his student, Fannie Pearl MacWilliams (one of the older students), fell in love. Even Fannie Pearl's subsequent move to finish school in Marshallberg, North Carolina, couldn't stand in the way of their growing relationship. They continued to see each other, despite the fact that the trip from the island to Marshallberg was a little over fifty miles. And that included the ferry ride. But their love grew, and in 1911, they were married.

Not long after their wedding, Stanley accepted a teaching position in Norfolk, Virginia. And soon after the move, seventeen-year-old Fannie Pearl MacWilliams Wahab discovered she was going to have a baby. In those days, it was not uncommon for women to stay with their family until their baby was born, so Fannie Pearl went back to Ocracoke Island and stayed with her husband's mother, Martha Ann Howard Wahab. And as the old saying goes, everything was fine until it wasn't.

One morning, Fannie Pearl woke up with an overwhelming sense of deep sorrow. She tried to put the feeling aside and get on with her day, but the feeling was just too strong. Finally, she told her mother-in-law about the horrible dream she'd had the night before. In the dream, she had watched herself die. Martha Ann agreed that would have been horrible. But

Fannie Pearl said there was something more—something even worse. In the nightmare, she'd seen herself dressed in white, lying in a white casket, and moving silently along the water in a white sailboat.

Unable to look away, she'd watched as the sailboat made its unearthly voyage along the silent, glittering waterway. Fannie Pearl's terror had increased with each passing moment until she'd finally awoken in a sweat. Gasping for breath, she felt as if the room were closing in on her. For the rest of the day, all she could think about was her body in the coffin, the full moon, and her journey into the unknown. The macabre images flashed through her mind hour after hour, no matter

what she did. Fannie worried there was nothing she could do to break the nightmare's hold on her.

The next night, Fannie Pearl MacWilliams Wahab died, as did the child she carried. As soon as their deaths were confirmed, her family and friends tried everything they could to contact Stanley Wahab to tell him about the tragic death of his wife and child. There were no phones on the island, but the coast guard was finally able to reach Stanley via a ship-to-shore phone call. Though Stanley was heartbroken, he told the family he would make the preparations and asked them not to do anything until he arrived on the island.

Stanley bought a beautiful casket, wanting something fine enough to honor the woman he loved. He made arrangements to ride to the island on the mail boat alongside his precious cargo, though he wouldn't arrive on Ocracoke Island until the next day. Once the casket was loaded and Stanley on board, the boat left the dock for the somber trip to Ocracoke.

Let's pause here a moment because it will be helpful to understand how things were done in those days. During Stanley's time, bodies were buried as soon as possible because there was no way to embalm a body on the island (embalming means to preserve a body from decay by treating it with special chemicals). And since his wife had been dead more than twenty-four hours, it was important that she be buried *right away*. In fact, the rest of the preparations moved so fast once Stanley arrived on Ocracoke, Martha Ann hadn't yet had a chance to

tell her son about Fannie Pearl's nightmare. So, there was nothing she could do but keep quiet and watch as they put Fannie Pearl MacWilliams Wahab's body in the beautiful solid white casket *that* her husband had purchased.

With Fannie Pearl's body ready for burial, they still had to get her to the cemetery. And since Fannie's burial plot was on a part of the island near her father's store and dock, it would mean carrying her coffin down long, sandy lanes and across planks and foot bridges that crossed the smaller creeks (called "guts"), all the way to the other side of the harbor.

As heartbroken as he was, Stanley still couldn't ask people to carry the coffin by hand across such challenging terrain. So, Stanley placed the white casket on a white skiff and started across the creek, while family, friends, and other members of the funeral procession followed in rowboats. And there beneath the night sky, illuminated by a full moon, Fannie Pearl MacWilliams Wahab was carried to her final resting place, dressed in white, in a white casket, and on board a white sailing skiff, exactly the way it had happened in her dream.

Here's a question for you: Did Fannie Pearl dream about her own death . . . or did she *scare* herself to death? What do you think?

Today, because of the popularity of dark tourism (traveling to places known for tragic historical events, or places associated with death) and some people's fascination with true stories of the supernatural, Fannie Pearl's grave is marked with a "No Trespassing" sign to keep people from trying to recreate their own paranormal experience at her final resting place. Maybe that will help her rest in peace.

The McDowell Columns Building, Chowan University

CHAPTER 4

The Haunted Town

While Murfreesboro is more of the "Inner Banks" of North Carolina, its short distance to the coast and sheer number of paranormal locations and events makes it a perfect addition to our tour of North Carolina's spooky coast. And in the case of Murfreesboro, more than just a few landmarks seem to be haunted. In this case, *the whole town* is a haven for supernatural activity. There are very few places you can go in Murfreesboro that are not haunted or free from eerie tales of strange occurrences.

William Hardy Murfree, an Irish immigrant, purchased a large tract of land in 1746, which became Murfree's Landing. Shortly after it was established, the site became a "King's Landing," where representatives of the king had the right to inspect all goods coming in and going out of the port by ship.

As the port prospered, so did the surrounding area. But all was not well in the town now known as Murfreesboro. Tuberculosis, the Spanish flu, and polio had taken their toll through the years, as had the Revolutionary War, the Civil War, and other tragedies. Still, Murfreesboro adapted and ultimately thrived. But even as things returned to normal, the town became a haven for the paranormal. Don't believe me? Come on. We'll take a short tour around town.

The Brown Lady

Chowan University began its existence as Chowan Baptist Female Institute. The school kept the name until 1910 when it became known as Chowan College. In 2006, the former college became Chowan University. Over the years, the institution produced professional athletes, business leaders, and politicians. But perhaps the most famous former student attended the school in 1886, and she still visits the campus every year in October—on Halloween. She is dressed in the same brown taffeta dress that she favored when she lived on campus. Her name is Eolene Davidson, but she is better known at Chowan University and around town as the "Brown Lady." Oddly enough, history had almost forgotten her name, and even today, the cause of her death is still uncertain. But every October 31, when she makes her ghostly return to campus,

Eolene's story comes back into sharp focus.

Eolene attended the college when it was still the Chowan Baptist Female Institute. She lived in the Columns Building and was known for wearing brown taffeta everywhere. In 1915, a student named Jessie Maie Piland wrote, "Among the many fair-haired and energetic girls that were preparing for college this beautiful September was Eolene Davidson, the beautiful daughter of a well-known farmer. She was a pleasant, sweet-natured girl of nineteen, tall and slender, with wavy black hair, fair complexion, and dreamy blue eyes."

Still, while we know her name and the fact that she was very popular, Eolene's death remains a mystery. The most cited account says she went to visit a friend in New York City, where she met a young attorney named James Lorrene. They fell in love, and James proposed. Eolene agreed to marry him, but she wanted to finish her education first. So, she returned to college and resumed her studies. Sadly, Eolene contracted typhoid fever in early October of her sophomore year. As she lay dying in her bed, friends told her fiancé about her condition. He made the trip to Murfreesboro from New York as fast as was possible in those days. Sadly, though, he arrived on November 1—he was too late. Eolene had died the night before on October 31st. Halloween.

But . . . is that what really happened? In another version of the story, Eolene met and fell in love with a handsome young soldier while in college. As in the first version, they made plans to marry. All was well as Eolene went about her days studying and spending time with friends (always dressed in her usual brown taffeta), until the news came that her fiancé had been killed. As the story goes, the news of his death was so devastating that

Eolene died that very night from a broken heart. A few other accounts say that when she heard the news, Eolene jumped to her death from the dormitory's roof, her handkerchief fluttering slowly to the ground and landing near her lifeless body. (I think it might have been the second version. How about you?)

However poor Eolene died, the stories all say it happened on Halloween. To this day, the Brown Lady makes her presence known by turning lights on and off and opening and closing doors. And if you listen carefully, you will most likely hear her footsteps—and possibly the swish and rustle of brown taffeta—on the third floor of the Columns Building, all on the anniversary of her Halloween death.

But don't think she's the only ghostly resident of the University. In Belk Hall, a student died by suicide many years ago. Even today, people report an eerie presence in the room. It has even been said that some previous occupants of the room have gone crazy there. And if that's not enough ghostly students hanging around for you, take a walk through campus to Mixon Hall (close to Garrison Stadium, the university's football stadium). Sometimes, people see the spectral shape of a young man roaming the second floor, said to be the same young man who hanged himself from the staircase in the residence hall many years ago.

One last undead resident "lives" in Daniel Hall (the music hall). This specter can most often be found playing the piano in one of the rooms. But it's best to listen from outside, because if you bravely decide to enter during the performance . . . there won't be anyone at the piano.

Brady C. Jefcoat Museum

In 1922, the building that is now the Brady C. Jefcoat Museum at 201 West High Street, was a school. And before Mr. Jefcoat was ever associated with the building, it was already a center of paranormal activity. For example, about forty years after the school opened, Marjorie Riddick was teaching her ninth-grade class when something odd happened. Mrs. Riddick was popular with her students and was fond of telling them stories about her family's haunted plantation home just north of town. One of Mrs. Riddick's former students talked about the day the "odd thing" happened: "Mrs. Riddick thought the ghosts followed her to school. The door came open, and she turned to the door and said, 'You just turn around and go back home. These students are in class now.' In a minute, the door closed, and she went right back to teaching without missing a beat!"

In the 1990s, the staff of the Murfreesboro Historical Association learned that a collection of antique music boxes, photographs, old washing machines, and other interesting Americana-related artifacts from the period between the 1850s and 1950s was available. The owner of the collection was an older, somewhat eccentric man named Brady C. Jefcoat. Many famous museums wanted parts of the collection, but Mr. Jefcoat insisted that the entire collection be preserved.

Since no museum wanted all of it, he established an endowment for the collection. (An endowment is funds and/or property donated to an institution.) Then, in 1990, Brady Jefcoat was invited to give the commencement address at Chowan University. After the address, the president of the university was

able to bring Mr. Jefcoat and the Murfreesboro Historical Society together. Mr. Jefcoat offered to give the full collection to the Murfreesboro Historical Association because they offered to purchase and upgrade the former high school building to give the collection a new home.

The unique assortment of items includes everything from toasters, washing machines, and Daisy air rifles, to mousetraps, dairy equipment, and even an X-ray machine that was used by shoe stores to accurately measure children's feet. The collection contained more than eighteen thousand items, enough to fill the newly renovated seventeen thousand square feet of display space. However, the story doesn't end there—not in a town as haunted as Murfreesboro. Even though the items have a new home and Mr. Jefcoat finally realized his dream of having his collection preserved intact, some people wonder if the eccentric former owner is still overseeing his possessions from beyond the grave, just as he did in life.

Is it possible that some of the items he collected have attracted a sort of residual paranormal energy? It could be. When looking at photographs of items in the collection, one stands out. The photograph shows what appears to be a crystal ball in which a face is reflected. Members of the Murfreesboro Historical Association have looked for an explanation and have even tried to replicate the phenomenon, but they have been unsuccessful on both counts. Their next course of action was to call on the Ghost Guild of North Carolina to conduct an investigation. The results should be interesting.

Death at Parker's Ferry

On November 16, 1924, Berry Credit, Odell Smith, Sarah Pope, Maggie Smith, Essie Smith, and Roberta Smith made the trip from Suffolk, Virginia to Roxobel, North Carolina, in a Ford Model T touring car, something of a luxury car in the 1920s. They had been looking forward to the trip to visit relatives who lived in the little North Carolina town, about twenty-three miles south of Murfreesboro.

The family was looking forward to a day of visiting, laughing, reminiscing, and eating some good home cooking with their family. They talked excitedly about the good time they were going to have. And by all accounts, the reunion was a happy one. But after their visit, the trip took a dark turn. On their way home, the car and everyone in it ended up at the bottom of the Meherrin River at Parker's Ferry Road. For one hundred years, one question has remained a mystery: How did six Black family members in a luxury car end up dead at the bottom of the Meherrin River later that night?

The question is as much a mystery today as it was a century ago. What were six people doing at the ferry at 8:00 p.m., a time when the ferry was not running? How did the car manage to roll into the river, killing everyone inside? Why did they not follow their original route back home through Murfreesboro instead of heading toward the river? Did they see something? Did something see them? Will anyone ever know the answer?

Want to learn more about this haunted town? The nice people at the Murfreesboro Historical Association (www.murfreesboronc.org) will be happy to tell you more. Or better yet, take the tour and see for yourself . . . if you're not afraid.

CHAPTER 5

You Can't Have a Ghostly North Carolina Coast Book Without Pirates

When we think about pirates, most often we see them as brash rogues who lived life on the edge, their exploits spawning countless tales of danger and adventure. The legends painted them as rum-drinking rascals who went where they pleased and took what they wanted, sailing under the Jolly Roger. But the truth might surprise you.

Pirates were active primarily from the

1600s through the 1700s, and they particularly liked the coast of North Carolina. After all, it had an unguarded coastline with many hidden inlets and coves, making it the perfect place for pirates to hide. Tall oceanside dunes kept small islands out of sight, which meant pirates could attack seemingly out of nowhere *and* make a quick getaway once they had disabled and unloaded captured ships.

Another fascinating fact? During this particular period in swashbuckling history, it was quite possible that pirates on any given ship might not understand each other! Why do you think that might be? Well, often, pirate crews were made up of sailors from many different countries. A ship might have English, Dutch, French, and African crew members. It was not unusual for formerly enslaved people from the Caribbean and North America to join a pirate crew rather than return to a life of slavery.

And pirate crews were not as prejudiced as many other people of that era. A pirate captain was more than happy to welcome formerly enslaved people on board and initiate them into pirate life. On these ships, Black pirates could vote, carry weapons, and receive an equal share of the spoils, just like everyone else. In fact, a pirate ship was one of the few places a Black man could get power and money in the 1600s and 1700s.

There is a myth that says pirate crews were made up entirely of men—but that's not true. For example, Anne Bonny and Mary Read were two of the most famous (and ferocious) female pirates in history. And they were as fierce as any man who ever walked the deck of a ship.

Another famous female pirate was Jacquotte Delahaye. She came from a poor family and grew up in tragic circumstances, as did many people of her era. Her mother died giving birth to her brother, and later, her father was murdered. After his death, Jacquotte didn't have many options. So, she joined a pirate crew. To her credit, Jacquotte was a fast learner, and in her later years, she commanded a fleet of pirate ships. Jacquotte Delahaye was a striking figure when commanding her crew from the deck of her ship. She had eye-catching, flaming-red hair. That, coupled with the fact that she survived many dangerous encounters, earned her the nickname "Back from the Dead Red."

In 1656, with the help of hundreds of other pirates, she took over a small Caribbean Island called Tortuga. But her "new republic" didn't last long. Several years later, Jacquotte died in a shoot-out while defending the island.

Even so, she is not the only pirate who had a reputation for "coming back from the dead."

The legendary pirate Blackbeard (real name: Edward Teach) was hunted down by Lieutenant Robert Maynard and captured at Ocracoke Inlet off the coast of North Carolina on November 22, 1718. During the ferocious battle that ensued, Maynard killed the notorious pirate. When the battle was over and Maynard examined Blackbeard's body, he noted that the pirate had been shot five times and cut (during a cutlass duel between Blackbeard and Maynard) about *twenty* times.

Maynard had Blackbeard's head cut off and his body thrown overboard. But Maynard wanted other pirates to know their days were numbered. So, he put Blackbeard's head on a pole at the entrance to the Chesapeake Bay as a warning to other pirates—and it remained there for several years. But that's not the end of the story. Keep reading to find out just how restless the ghost of Blackbeard was—and still is.

CHAPTER 6

Blackbeard: King of the Pirates

Blackbeard—his name struck fear into the hearts of those who hunted for him, and especially anyone who crossed him. Although his real name was Edward Teach, the name Blackbeard became synonymous with the pirate life. He was tall, strong, and had a thick black beard (yep . . . that's where the name came from).

To make himself look even scarier before a battle, he would plait the beard into little pigtails, tie them with colored ribbons, and twist braids behind his ears. Immediately before battle, he would light several long, slow-burning hemp cords and tuck them under his hat, allowing wisps of smoke to curl up around his face. He also wore pistols, daggers, and a cutlass in a belt about his waist. He wore a sling that held six pistols across his chest, all of them primed, cocked, and ready to fire.

But Edward Teach had not always been a pirate. Originally, he had been a sailor based out of Jamaica during the War of the Spanish Succession. So, what caused him to make the transition from soldier and British privateer (someone who commanded a privately owned armed ship commissioned by a hostile state to attack enemy ships) to *Blackbeard*, the most feared pirate on the seven seas? Well, from what we know, he joined Benjamin Hornigold's crew in 1716. Soon, Edward Teach was in charge of a sloop (a small warship popular among pirates for its size and speed) he had captured, and a crew of approximately seventy men.

On November 28, 1717, Teach attacked a French merchant vessel, *La Concorde*, off the coast of Saint Vincent and, in the course of the attack, forced the captain to surrender.

At this point, he no longer went by the name Edward Teach. He was Blackbeard. He renamed the ship *Queen Anne's Revenge* and equipped it with forty guns. (Now here's an odd fact. Though his ship was formidable, and he had the reputation of being scary and ruthless, there is no historical evidence of Blackbeard having ever murdered or harmed anyone.)

Blackbeard pillaged ships from the Caribbean to the Carolinas. In fact, he even had a residence called Blackbeard's Castle on the island of St. Thomas in the Caribbean. But North Carolina was the place he called home toward the end of his career. In September 1718, Blackbeard hosted the largest gathering of pirates ever assembled in North America. The gathering took place at what is now called Teach's Hole (near Ocracoke Inlet). The pirates sang, danced, ate, and drank a whole lot of rum. The party lasted for days and only ended when the food and rum ran out. As it turned out, this would be Blackbeard's final celebration.

The governor of Virginia, Alexander Spotswood, sent Lieutenant Robert Maynard of the British Royal Navy to track down the notorious pirate and end his reign of terror on the high seas. On November 22, 1718, Maynard caught up with Blackbeard in a deep-water channel just offshore of Springer's Point. The ensuing battle was a bloodbath by all accounts. Those on the pirate's crew who weren't killed were captured. In the end, Blackbeard took twenty-five wounds from bullets, a sword, and a dagger before Maynard's cutlass slashed through his massive neck.

Maynard took Blackbeard's head and hung it on the bowsprit of his ship. Then, he pushed the body of the notorious pirate into the sea. But what happened next truly shocked the Lieutenant's terrified crew. Legend has it that Blackbeard's head cried, "Come on, Edward," from where it hung on the bowsprit. And the pirate's headless body swam around the ship three times before plunging beneath the waves.

Now, if you're ever in the place called Teach's Hole at night, you might just have some company. Because Teach's headless ghost can sometimes be seen swimming just below the water surface in the vicinity of his

last battle . . . looking for his head. On windy nights, people have seen a strange light, called "Teach's Light," coming from the direction of the Pamlico Sound. Then they hear a voice, carried on the wind, saying, "*Where is my head?*"

CHAPTER 7

Ghost Ships and Their Undead Crews

Sometimes they appear as ghostly images on the horizon. Though you can chase them, you'll never catch them. But sometimes, if you're unlucky enough to be near one, you can smell the mold and brine, and even see the undead crews as they make their way across eternity. Just between you and me, I don't want to be quite that close.

While most ships that went down into the sea never to return simply stayed on the bottom, there are some "special" cases. Take, for example, the story of the *Crissie Wright*. On January 11, 1886, Captain Jeb Collins and his men were in the fight of their lives just off the coast of North Carolina. Ice had frozen the rigging, so the men had to lower the sails. Conditions were so bad, even trying to walk on the deck was dangerous.

Waves hammered the ship, and between the extreme cold and the relentless pounding of the sea, the ship began to flounder (no pun intended). The sailors' fingers and toes were frozen, so even holding on was almost impossible. Some held on for dear life, while others lost the battle and were swept overboard into the freezing, churning water. Then a monster wave smashed onto the deck and broke the mast in half! The debris from the impact punched a hole through the deck.

Less than a minute later, the remainder of the mast broke with a crack like thunder. It drove through the deck and the hull, and the ship went down. There were no survivors. And yet . . . somehow . . . the ship sails on. When the weather is rough and the waves are pounding the shore, you can see the *Crissie Wright* and its ghost crew still battling the waves, just as they have done for centuries.

But some ghost ships are not so obvious. Just south of Topsail Island, where I used to live, near a place called Rich Inlet, there's a spot where a ghost ship waits. Fishermen and pleasure boaters have both seen the

phenomenon. If you ever have the opportunity to be on a boat in that area, watch the marine radar unit closely. Many people have reported seeing an image that looks like the presence of a ship, yet the coast is completely clear. No ships in sight. Even so, the radar often shows the ghost ship pursuing boats for a while. And almost as suddenly as it appeared, the mark fades.

Like it was never there at all.

Is it a technological glitch of some kind? Probably not, since it happens on so many different radar units at different times. It's possible the ghost ship makes its presence known, then returns to the spectral realm, leaving startled sailors and fishermen to look around in amazement.

But that's just the tip of the iceberg, so to speak. North Carolina has some of the most famous ghost ships and ghostly ship residents in the world. And not all of them are from centuries past. Come on. I'll show you.

The *Carroll A. Deering*

Some ships sail from one destination to another with little or no problem. Just another routine trip in a series of routine trips. But sometimes, every once in a while, a ship comes up against something completely unexplainable. Maybe even otherworldly. The *Carroll A. Deering* is just such a ship. And one hundred years later, we still have more questions than answers.

On January 29, 1921, the *Carroll A. Deering* was making a return trip to Hampton Roads, Virginia from Barbados, when it passed the Cape Lookout Lightship. According to the lightship keeper, the crew was milling about when a crewman, who did not look or act like an officer, reported that the ship had lost its anchors. The following day, the ship passed the SS *Lake Elon* southwest of the Diamond Shoals Lightship at approximately 5:45 p.m. The *Deering* seemed to be steering a peculiar course. This was the last report of the ill-fated *Deering* before it was found run aground and abandoned.

Early on January 31, C. P. Brady of the Cape Hatteras Coast Guard Station spotted the five-masted schooner floundering helpless on the shoals. The sails were set and the lifeboats were missing. The ship seemed to be abandoned. Due to heavy seas, the surf boats failed to reach the wreck, and it would be days before anyone could. In the early morning hours of February 4, the wrecker *Rescue* and the cutter *Manning* finally reached the battered ship. After an investigation of the *Deering*, it was discovered that all personal belongings, key navigational equipment, certain papers, and the ship's anchors were missing. Then things really got strange. Food was laid out as if in preparation for a meal. Except . . . there was no sign of the crew.

Even the Library of Congress, in its *Headlines and Heroes* publication, had questions about the ill-fated voyage but few answers.

As speculation sailed through the pages of newspapers and government investigations, comparisons were made to other mysterious nautical disappearances. Still within recent memory for many was the disappearance three years earlier of the USS *Cyclops,* along with all passengers and crew—nearly three hundred people had gone missing. The *Cyclops*, a nineteen thousand collier took a similar route to the *Deering*—departure from Brazil, a stop in Barbados, and then up the U.S. coast. The ship left on March 4, 1989 on a trip that should have taken no more than nine days. Could it have been sunk by a German ship as part of hostilities in the First World War? Again, no evidence was ever found to provide us with answers.

In a similar case, the SS *Hewitt*, a steel-hulled bulk freighter, left fully loaded from Sabine Pass, Port Arthur, Texas, on January 20, 1921. It was bound for Portland, Maine, with a stop in Boston, Massachusetts. It was last seen 250 nautical miles north of Jupiter Inlet, Florida—at which point, the ship and its entire crew disappeared without a trace.

"What did the *Carroll A. Deering*, USS *Cyclops,* and the *Hewitt* have in common? In addition to the missing people, *they all passed over that mysterious stretch of ocean known as the Bermuda Triangle*. Myths about the Bermuda Triangle wouldn't start until some forty years later, but the ghost ship *Carroll A. Deering* is still discussed as one of its many mysteries."

What we know for sure is that the wrecked and battered hull of the *Deering* was all that was left to signify the vessel's strange passage. In March 1921, as the vessel began breaking apart on the shoals, it was towed away and then dynamited. The ongoing interest in the *Deering* mystery may be due to the many historical threads uncovered in the investigation of this amazing story.

Agent Thompson of the FBI visited Dare County in July 1921. When he asked local coast guardsmen about the theory that the crew had mutinied and abandoned ship before striking the shoals, they responded, "Impossible!" The coast was too rough for lifeboat landings. In the end, the investigation proved fruitless. No trace of the crew, the ship's log, or the navigation equipment has ever been discovered.

The Flaming Ship of Ocracoke

Some eerie events are as much a part of history as the flight of the Wright Brothers airplane (1903) or the signing of the Declaration of Independence (1776). Maybe that's what makes them so terrifying. For example, because of the religious wars that raged throughout Europe in the late seventeenth and early eighteenth centuries, many refugees were being driven from their various homelands. As the situation worsened, the new King and Queen of England (William of Orange and his wife, Mary) accepted thousands of these refugees, allowing many to start new lives in the North Carolina colonies.

Even so, there was still the problem of providing them safe passage to the colonies. Christoph von Graffenried, a Swiss baron, offered a solution. He would escort a large number of these refugees to the settlement of New Bern in the Carolina colonies. Most of the crossings took the refugees with no problem. But the one ship that sailed during the new moon in September would prove to be a death ship.

Its captain was a dangerous and greedy man, and as the passengers boarded the ship, he noticed that the group was carrying large amounts of gold and jewels. These items were the refugees' family treasures, brought from their various homelands. But the greedy captain had plans for the treasures . . . and the passengers.

On a dark and moonless night, as the ship drew closer to the Outer Banks of North Carolina, the captain and his bloodthirsty crew crept below decks and, one by one, slit the throat of each passenger while they slept. Then, after making sure every passenger was dead,

the crew loaded the treasure on the ship's longboat and set the ship on fire.

Flames roared against the night sky as the captain and his crew rowed the longboat toward the town of Bath. As they made their way to their hideout, the pirates laughed about the dead travelers and bragged about how rich they were going to be. Little did they know, something not of this world had other plans. Before long, the captain turned and looked behind them. And what he saw made his blood run cold.

The doomed ship had begun to move. Its sails were in flaming tatters, and even though there wasn't any wind, the ship was sailing toward them at full speed. Even MORE frightening? No living person was steering this ship. Instead, a spectral crew made up of those who had been murdered in their sleep sailed closer, and *closer*. As the pirates screamed in terror, the flaming ship rammed the longboat, sending it, the treasure, and the murderers to the bottom of the sea.

The next day, the burned-out ship washed ashore on Ocracoke Island. And now, over three hundred years later, locals still say that if you scan the horizon off Ocracoke Island on the night of the new moon in September, you might just see the outline of a flaming ship manned by an undead crew . . . making its way silently toward the island.

The USS *North Carolina*

In a book of spooky stories like this, it is not often you have such excellent, firsthand expert experience to draw from. But we do. So, settle back and get ready to tour the Battleship *North Carolina* and meet some of its ghostly inhabitants! But first, just a little history (I promise, just a little). The ship was the first vessel of its type built for the United States Navy. And it was the most decorated battleship of World War II.

After the attack on Pearl Harbor in 1941, the *North Carolina* was transferred to the Pacific to strengthen the Allied forces. The *North Carolina* operated briefly off the East Coast in 1946 before being decommissioned. Instead of being dismantled and scrapped, the ship was saved and preserved as a museum ship in Wilmington, North Carolina. And that's where it still sits today, a silent sentinel on the Cape Fear River. But unlike many such ships, at the end of the day, when the tourists have headed back to their hotels and the staff has gone home, the USS *North Carolina* is not quite . . . empty.

In October 2020, Danielle Wallace (Battleship *North Carolina* programs director), Nelson Nauss (executive director/cofounder of the Ghost Guild Inc. www.theghostguild.com), and Jon Michael (investigator with the Ghost Guild Inc.) were part of a program on the haunted battleship presented at the North Carolina Museum of History. Daniele Wallace told the gathered crowd about her first ghostly encounters on the ship.

When you live in Wilmington, you hear the stories about the battleship being haunted, and I came on board thinking, "Okay, I'm going to play along, and if people ask me, I'm going to say, 'Oh, yeah, it's haunted.'" And this is until I saw the ghosts myself. The first time, I was participating in an EFP session down in the sick bay area with my coworker, Shelly, and we saw this dark-blue, dark-purple orb just hanging over this particular bed. And when I said to the gentleman, the lead investigator, to please take a picture of that area, he did so. And as soon as he pulled his camera out, it was gone.

I hadn't said anything to Shelly, but she whispered to me, "Oh, I saw that, too." But that was the first time. The second time was when I saw the Shadow Man in the mess decks of the battleship. I was talking to someone late at night. We were getting ready for an event called Ghost Ship, which is where we turned the ship into a haunted house for Halloween. It was just me and one other gentleman on board. I was talking to him, and I could see over his shoulder the Shadow Man. Just sort of walked past, and after a few minutes, he walked back across. The thing about the battleship is that things are completely still and quiet at night. Things don't move around. Well, nothing except the Shadow Man.

The battleship's reputation for being haunted is not limited to North Carolina. A few years before Danielle's Shadow Man sighting, the ship was the site of a private event. The event included an opportunity for members to meet Jason Hawes and Grant Wilson from the TV show *Ghost Hunters*. They flew in the night before and arranged to meet Danielle on board the ship at about 10:00 p.m. But this was not for the show. Jason and Grant had heard stories about the haunted battleship and just wanted to experience it for themselves with no one else around.

On one occasion, Nelson Nauss was in the communications area of the ship. Wes, a regular on many investigations, was there and accounted for. "So, we were in this area, and we were doing an EVP (Electronic Voice Phenomenon) recording, when all of a sudden, you hear this thing in the background. And what's interesting about this is not an EVP. It's not something that was just recorded on our recorders and that we didn't hear. This was audible. We both heard it with our own ears." When the clip plays, the words are very distinct: "There's no reason to hide from us."

But the ghosts were not through communicating. Ghost Guild member Kelly had an interesting encounter in the brig.

The first time I investigated the brig at the USS North Carolina, *I remember walking in and getting this immediate sensation like I was being watched . . . And since I was in the brig where the naughty battleship boys would have been placed, I said, "I like the bad boys. If you were a bad boy, can you light up my RemPod?" (RemPod is short for Radiating Electro-Magnetic Pod, a device designed to detect fluctuations in electromagnetic fields.) Sure enough, my RemPod starts flashing and making all kinds of noise . . .So, I asked my spirit, "Would you like me to sing you a song?" And my RemPod lit up again.*

I started singing. "Of all the boys I've known, and I've known some / Until I first met you, I was lonesome." And

then I would stop, and I would say, "If you want me to keep going, light up my machine." And it would light up. At the end of the song, I said, "Now, if you really liked my singing, please light up my machine." And it lit up.

Made me feel pretty good. So, I asked a few more questions, but the night was moving along, and so it was time for me to go. I said to the guy, "Hey, it's time for me to leave. If you want me to come back and visit you again sometime, can you light my machine up one last time?" Sure enough, it lit up. But this time, after it lit up, I watched a ball of light come up out of the machine and shoot into the cell next to it. I had never seen anything like it.

Yes, even though the battleship has been docked for decades, the ship is pretty active. Pot lids bang and benches move in the mess hall. Bed springs creak in the sick bay almost on command. When investigators asked the entity that was making the springs creak if it could make the noise louder, there was a brief pause, followed by a loud THUD—as if someone had jumped on the bed. As The Ghost Guild investigators told me, this particular manifestation is significant because a physical force had to make the bed springs move.

I have visited the Battleship *North Carolina* a number of times, but never at night. How about you? Would you like to search for the spirits on board the ship? Maybe hang out in the brig or the galley? If you're scared to visit a haunted ship all by yourself, just remember: You probably won't be alone for very long!

The Gray Man of Hatteras

This last tale is more of a warning than a story. Having lived on an island just off the coast of North Carolina for a while, I can tell you, when hurricanes and tropical storms hit, it's best to be prepared. And there is one foolproof way to know if foul weather is afoot.

Hurricanes are a way of life on Hatteras Island. Though the Atlantic hurricane season runs from June 1 through November 30, the strongest storms typically impact the North Carolina coast between mid-August and September. Cape Hatteras, an island in the long chain of barrier islands that make up North Carolina's Outer Banks, is a prime target for hurricanes, tropical storms, nor'easters, and other severe storms—thanks to its location right on the edge of the Gulf Stream, just off the state's east coast. As such, the locals are very familiar with the National Weather Service, NOAA, and other severe-weather tracking agencies. But another source tells them exactly how bad a storm will be. He's the

Gray Man, and as many people in this part of North Carolina will tell you, he's *never* wrong.

The Gray Man is often seen walking in the shadow of the Cape Hatteras Lighthouse or in other areas along the shore, and his presence is a warning that bad weather is approaching. The shadowy, indistinct figure has been around since the early 1900s. He normally arrives with the first light winds of a storm. But he never appears for minor weather systems. No, a sighting of the Gray Man means the island is in for a rough time.

Who is this mysterious Gray Man of Hatteras? Some say he is the spirit of someone who was terrorized by a storm. Though he didn't survive, he stays to warn others so they won't share his tragic fate. Others believe him to be the ghost of a sailor originally from the island who returns to warn others about impending storms. And still others say he was never a man at all. Not human, not a ghost or a spirit, but a force of nature generated by the storm itself.

Though you might say the Gray Man is a spectral fixture around Cape Hatteras, he has been seen as far away as Pawleys Island, South Carolina. There is even video of him in that area just before Hurricane Florence. However, the Gray Man never speaks; he's usually just seen calmly walking near the shore. Wherever he is and whatever he is, it's always best to heed his warning and keep your distance. Witnesses say if you approach him, he will disappear. But then again, so should *you* . . . unless you're ready to ride out a storm like you've never seen before . . . what the locals call a real frog strangler.

Weeping Arch Gate

Quick Spooky Facts

Cedar Grove Cemetery Weeping Arch: The triple-arched gateway at the Queen Street entrance of Cedar Grove Cemetery in New Bern is beautiful. It is made of coquina, also known as "shell stone." But the massive stone gateway also holds a mysterious secret. It's always dry until a funeral procession passes through the arch. Then water begins to drip, as if the arch is weeping. Sometimes the water is clear, and sometimes, it has a reddish tint—like blood. But it *only* drips during funeral processions.

Some people say if the water drips on a person, they will be the next to die. Is the arch a harbinger of death? And here's the real question: Would you dare to walk beneath it?

Dymond City Lights: Dymond City was never a large town, but by 1885, it had a hotel, a school, and houses for the railroad and lumber yard workers and their families. But after the old-growth timber was depleted and a second railroad line was built nearby, the town began to die. By 1920, the post office had closed, and in 1927, the town caught fire. Its houses, hotel, and everything else burned down, and within a few years, the forest finished the job. The town of Dymond City no longer existed—at least not in the way it once had.

Today, the road leading to what was once Dymond City comes to an intersection. One side is gated and closed to the public. But the other side . . . that's where strange things have been known to happen. On that side of the intersection, people report seeing lights bobbing up and down in the woods, or a fireball moving above the trees. Some say they are the ghosts of railroad men faithfully manning their posts from a railroad gone one hundred years. Others say it is the people of the former Dymond City who can't—or *won't*—leave their beloved home. What do you think it is? If you ever find yourself where Dymond City used to be, keep your eyes on those dark woods. You just might spot something otherworldly dancing between the trees.

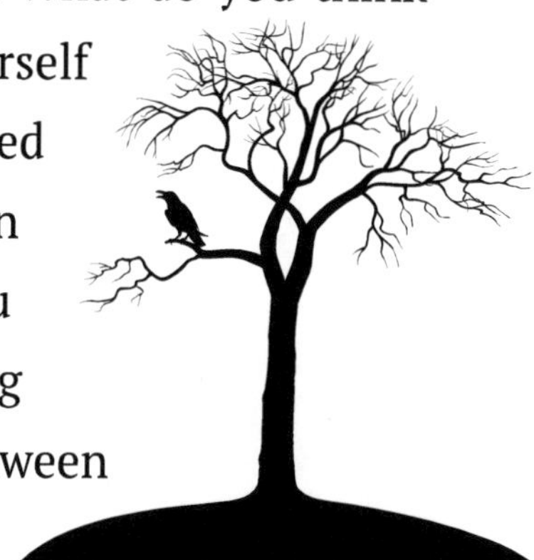

The Cotton Exchange: Often, when a place is said to be haunted, there's a story or tragic event that helps explain why. But here's something strange: The Cotton Exchange is full of ghosts, even though nothing spooky has happened there! (At least, nothing anyone knows of.) Take the specter called Fred, for example. For 150 years, he has appeared at night dressed all in black, his long, curly hair floating in the breeze—even when there isn't one. He is known to sneak up behind shop patrons and breathe down their necks.

Then there's the Lady in the White Dress. She likes to hang out at the German Café (especially at the top of the stairs in the upper dining room) and in Fidler's Gallery.

The Cotton Exchange has other ghostly visitors, too. People in old-fashioned Victorian clothes have a tendency to appear and then vanish near where the Fire and Spice Gourmet Shop used to be. And there's even a ghost dressed in a suit and top hat who is evidently a music lover. He's often seen standing at the listening station near Golden Gallery.

The saddest spirit is the soldier. He is usually seen around Port City Pottery in his blue uniform with a gold braid. But unlike the other ghosts, he doesn't move things around or make lights flicker. He just wants someone to talk to. As the story goes, he once asked a visitor, "Why do people keep walking by me? I just want to tell my story to someone."

Last but not least, there are the two little girls who love to play pranks. One spends most of her time in Top Toad, knocking over displays and unplugging various items. The other little girl hangs out at the Scoop, where she pours syrup on the counter, tips over stacks of plates, and plays with the wind chimes. She has even been known to turn the microwave, blender, radio, and mixer on and off when nobody is looking.

But here's the puzzling part: *Why*? What attracts the undead to the Cotton Exchange? It was never the site of slavery, murder, corruption, nor any other event that would make it hard for spirits to move on. What do you think draws them to the site? Do you think the Scoop serves Ice-Scream and Ladyfinger Cake? The truth is, we may never know. Maybe the ghosts just know a good spooky spot when they see one.

A Ghostly Goodbye

Well, fellow ghost hunters, that was some trip. Between ghost ships and their undead crews, a pirate still searching for his head, an arch that weeps blood, and even an entire haunted town, we have just about seen it all.

But that's not everything by any means. There are ghostly specters and spooky happenings all *over* the North Carolina coast. Maybe even where you live. Do you know any good ghost stories from your town or city? If you do, that might be a good way to start your own ghost hunting adventures. Maybe even start your own Ghost Hunters Club. And if you do, remember these important things:

Be safe. Always ask permission before visiting any spooky sites (remember, some places like Fannie MacWilliams's grave are marked "No Trespassing"). Don't go by yourself; use the buddy system. Always be respectful of the sites you visit, and write down

what you see and hear. Who knows? You might just want to write your own spooky stories later.

Thank you for taking this trip with me along North Carolina's haunted coast. Did you learn some new spooky stories to tell your friends? Maybe we'll meet again sometime. I have more stories to tell.

Well, it's getting late and the fog is rolling in. There's also a strange sort of light out in the mist. Perfect conditions for ghost hunting. I think I'll grab the binoculars and take a look along the horizon first.

What do you think I'll see?

And—do you think it will see me?

Thomas Smith has been a writer for many years and his favorite stories are the spooky ones. If it has haunted houses, creepy graveyards, ghost ships, or specters in the moonlight, he'll read it. He even lived in a haunted house for a couple of years (but the ghost was friendly, so they got along fine). Now he lives at the beach in Florida with his wife, six guitars, and a sock monkey named Ray. You can learn more about him at www.thomas-smith.us.

Check out some of the other *Spooky America* titles available now!

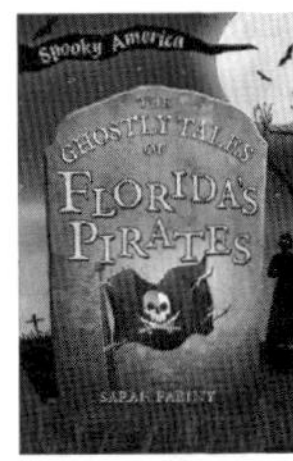

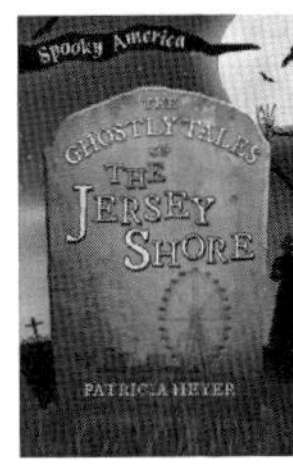

Spooky America was adapted from the creeptastic *Haunted America* series for adults. *Haunted America* explores historical haunts in cities and regions across America. Here's more from the original *Haunted North Carolina Coast* author, Thomas Smith: